I0876104

rockschool®

Ukulele

US Level 3 (UK Grade 3)

Performance pieces, technical exercises, supporting tests and in-depth guidance for Rockschool assessments

All accompanying and supporting audio can be downloaded from: *www.rslawards.com/downloads*

Input the following code when prompted: **AB448K9L3D**

For more information, turn to page 5

www.rslawards.com

Acknowledgements

Published by RSL Awards Ltd. © 2020
Catalogue Number: RSK200128US
ISBN: 978-1-78936-177-3
Initial US Release | Errata details can be found at *www.rslawards.com/errata*

SYLLABUS
Syllabus designed and written by Jono Harrison
Syllabus Director: Tim Bennett-Hart
Syllabus Consultants: Ashley Hards and Samantha Muir
Hit Tune arrangements by Ashley Hards, Giorgio Serci, Jono Harrison, Calum Harrison & Nat Martin
Supporting Tests written by Jono Harrison and Ashley Hards

PUBLISHING
Proof reading of arrangements by Jono Harrison, Ashley Hards & Calum Harrison
Music engraving, book layout and cover updates by Simon Troup and Jennie Troup of Digital Music Art
Fact files written and edited by Abbie Thomas
Proof reading and copy editing by Jono Harrison, Calum Harrison & Rosie Howard
Cover design by Philip Millard of Rather Nice Design
Cover photograph: © Olga Yatsenko (Shutterstock)

AUDIO
Produced by Jono Harrison
Mixed by Ian Caple & Jono Harrison
Engineered by Jono Harrison, Rory Harvey, Pete Riley, Giorgio Serci and Nat Martin
Supporting Tests recorded by Jono Harrison & Andy Robertson

MUSICIANS
Ukulele: Giorgio Serci, Samantha Muir, Nat Martin, Jono Harrison, Rory Harvey & Calum Harrison
Piano and Keyboards: Jono Harrison & Rory Harvey
Drums & Percussion: Pete Riley
Bass & Synth Bass: Rory Harvey
Guitars: Rory Harvey & Jono Harrison
Lead and Backing Vocals: Nick Shirm, Glen Harvey & Katy Virgoe
Additional Programming: Rory Harvey & Jono Harrison

EXECUTIVE PRODUCERS
John Simpson and Norton York

DISTRIBUTION
Exclusive distributors: Hal Leonard

CONTACTING ROCKSCHOOL
www.rslawards.com
Telephone: +44 (0)345 460 4747
Email: *info@rslawards.com*

Awarding the Contemporary Arts

Table of Contents

Introductions & Information

Rockschool Level/Grade Pieces

Technical Exercises

Supporting Tests

About Rockschool Assessments

Additional Information

Welcome to Rockschool Ukulele Level/Grade 3

Welcome to Rockschool's contemporary Ukulele syllabus 2020. This syllabus is designed to support ukulele players in their progression from Debut up to Level/Grade 8, through an engaging and rigorous pathway covering all the genres, stylistic elements, techniques and musical skills required for success as a contemporary ukulele player.

All elements required to participate in a Rockschool assessment can be found in the level/grade book. These are as follows:

Hit Tune Arrangements

The 2020 syllabus comprises six hit tune arrangements, meticulously researched and benchmarked to meet level/grade standards. The arrangements are devised so as to equip contemporary ukulele players with industry-relevant skills in any performance environment. These include:

- **All Levels/Grades**
  Four *'Session Style'* arrangements – focussing on developing skills required to perform in an ensemble environment, either in the studio or on stage. These arrangements cover accompaniment and lead playing skills.

- **Debut – Level/Grade 3**
  Two *'Duet'* arrangements – instrumental arrangements without a backing band, focussing on melody and accompaniment skills. The duet arrangements have a second part for teaching/ensemble purposes.

- **Levels/Grades 4–8**
  Two *'Solo'* arrangements, performed without backing track and arranged to test melodic and self-accompaniment skills.

Each Hit Tune arrangement is preceded by a Fact File, giving surrounding context to the piece and the original performers /recording artists.

Furthermore, you will find performance notes giving additional supportive context to get the most out of the pieces.

Technical Exercises

These are divided into groups at all levels/grades as outlined below:

- **Debut – Level/Grade 5** | Divided into *three* groups:
  Group A: Scales
  Group B: Arpeggios
  Group C: Chords

- **Levels/Grades 6–8** | Divided into *four* groups:
  Group A: Scales
  Group B: Arpeggios
  Group C: Chords
  Group D: Stylistic Studies

Supporting Tests

There are three sections in this part of the assessment. Please note that the sections contain differing elements depending on the level/grade:

Section 1

Sight Reading *or* **Improvisation & Interpretation** | *Debut – Level/Grade 5 only*
At Debut to Level/Grade 5, candidates can choose between the following:

- **Sight Reading** – a test of the musician's ability to read and perform previously unseen material
- **Improvisation & Interpretation** – a test of the musician's ability to develop previously unseen material in a stylistic way and perform improvised passages of melody. The book contains examples of both types of test. Equivalent 'unseen' examples will be provided for the assessment.

Quick Study Piece | *Levels/Grades 6–8 only*
At Levels/Grades 6–8, candidates must perform a previously unseen Quick Study Piece, combining the skills of the Sight Reading and Improvisation & Interpretation tests from earlier levels/grades.

Section 2

Ear Tests
Candidates must take all tests in this section. Ear tests feature at all levels/grades, but the elements differ as outlined below:

- **Melodic Recall** *and* **Rhythmic Recall** tests | *Debut – Level/Grade 3*
- **Melodic Recall** *and* **Harmonic Recall** tests | *Levels/Grades 4–8*

Section 3

General Musicianship Questions
Candidates must answer General Musicianship Questions (GMQ's) at all levels/grades, on one of their chosen pieces from the repertoire section. The nature of the questions differs depending on the level/grade. Please refer to the relevant section of the level/grade book for details.

Audio

All accompanying audio can be downloaded from RSL directly at *www.rslawards.com/downloads*. This includes backing tracks and full mixes of the level/grade pieces, examples of the technical exercises and supporting tests, and click tracks (where applicable). The audio files are supplied as MP3 format, and can be played using any compatible device.

You will need to input this code when prompted: **AB448K9L3D**

Note: If you have purchased a digital version of this book, you will be sent a link through which you can download the accompanying audio.

'Perfect' | Ed Sheeran

Album: ÷
Released: 2017
Label: Asylum/Atlantic
Genre: Pop

Written By: Ed Sheeran
Produced By: Ed Sheeran, Will Hicks
Chart Peak: 1 (US Billboard Hot 100)

Background Info

'Perfect' was the fourth single to be released from Ed Sheeran's chart-topping album ÷ *(Divide)*. The track was well-received globally, topping the charts in both the UK and the US as well as an impressive sixteen other countries worldwide. 'Perfect' gave Sheeran his second UK number one single from the album, with 'Shape of You' already having topped the charts on its release. The first and third single releases, 'Castle on the Hill' and 'Galway Girl', followed closely behind and peaked at number two. 'Perfect' achieved incredible sales globally and was certified 4 x Platinum in the UK and 8 x Platinum in the US.

Despite it's later release, 'Perfect' was actually the first song to be written and destined for Sheeran's third studio album ÷ *(Divide)*. Inspired by and written for his girlfriend Cherry Seaborn, Sheeran was determined to create the greatest love song he'd ever write and to show his listeners his true sincerity. Feeling that his previous release, 'Thinking Out Loud', had come to define him, he wanted to create something even more heartfelt and emotional. Having successfully written the song, Sheeran set out to produce it with the help of Will Hicks (Grammy-nominated British producer) and instrumental assistance from his brother Matthew Sheeran. Until now the brothers had never collaborated together, but with their Grandmother being elderly they decided to fulfil her final wish which was to see them work together. In light of this, Matthew provided the strings orchestration for the recording of 'Perfect'.

The release of ÷ *(Divide)* saw Sheeran break Frankie Laine's 1953 record as he occupied all of the top five positions in the UK Singles chart and placed nine songs in the top ten. With an unbelievable reception worldwide, the singer-songwriter's album achieved certified status in a staggering 22 countries across the globe. With over three million sales in the UK he saw his album certified 11 x Platinum in his home country and with four million US sales he received 4 x Platinum status in America.

To date, Sheeran has sold more than 150 million records worldwide, making him one of the best-selling artists of all time. His second album, *'x'*, features on the list of the 100 best-selling UK albums in chart history, coming in at number 20.

Performance Notes

This slow pop ballad is written in the time signature of $\frac{12}{8}$ which means there are four beats in each measure but each beat is then divided into three rather than two. This triple division of notes is called compound time. It results in a steady four beat pulse with a gentle swaying feel. You play the accompaniment at the start and it is important to establish the feel and the mood in these opening measures.

You will be playing the melody for the verse and bridge, so take care with the balance of the melody and the accompaniment. You will need to be heard over the accompaniment whilst maintaining the gentle laid-back feel of the song. Make sure your phrases are of a similar feel to the original vocal line by thinking of your melody as musical sentences. A singer would need to breathe between phrases which naturally breaks up the melody. Notice that some notes are held at the end of phrases whereas others are cut short to provide space.

You can use your own choice of chord voicing and rhythm in chorus, marked by the accompaniment development section (measures 21 to 28). Try experimenting with strummed chords and arpeggios until you find the right feel to match the melody. The dynamics gradually increase through the song with the chorus section being marked as ***f*** *(forte)* however, you need to take care to compliment the second ukulele with your accompanying part. It must not be so loud or full that you over power it.

Perfect

Duet

Candidate Part (Assessed)

Ed Sheeran

Bridge
G
Em
C
mf
T
A
B
[13]
G
D
G
Em
[16]
C
D
[19]
Chorus
Em
C
G
D
Em
C
f Develop accompaniment
[21]
G
D
Em
C
G
D
[24]
Em
C
G
D
[27]
G
mf
[29]

Perfect

Duet

Duet Part (Non-assessed)

Ed Sheeran

G
Em
[17]
C
D
[19]
Chorus
Em
C
G
D
Em
C
f
[21]
G
D
Em
C
G
D
[24]
Em
C
G
D
[27]
G
[29]

'Viva La Vida' | Coldplay

Album: *Viva la Vida or Death and All His Friends*
Released: 2008
Label: Parlophone/Capitol
Genre: Pop/Rock

Written By: Guy Berryman, Jonny Buckland, Will Champion, Chris Martin
Produced by: Markus Dravs, Brian Eno, Jon Hopkins, Rik Simpson
Chart Peak: 1 (US)

Background Info

'Viva la Vida' was the second single to be released from Coldplay's fourth studio album, *Viva la Vida or Death and All His Friends*. On its release in May 2008 the track took the charts by storm and peaked at the top spot in both the UK and US, giving Coldplay their first single to achieve number 1 status in both countries. The hit was met with critical acclaim and achieved outstanding sales worldwide, becoming only the sixth song to sell over 4 million digital copies in the US.

'Viva la Vida' moved away from Coldplay's classic electric guitar or piano led song, with the most prominent instrumental part being that of a strings section. Davide Rossi, Italian composer, conductor and producer, arranged and conducted the string section for not only this track but also for several others that feature on *Viva la Vida or Death and All His Friends*. This has become some of his best-known commercial work, along with his contribution to The Verve's album, *Forth*, and for his time spent as an instrumentalist in electro-pop band Goldfrapp.The formation of Coldplay began when Chris Martin (lead vocals/piano) met Jonny Buckland (guitar) at University College London in 1996. The pair immediately hit it off and spent the entirety of their first year planning a rock band together. It took some time for the pair to achieve the line-up and image that they wanted, but in 2000 they finally released their debut album *Parachutes*, along with fellow bandmates Guy Berryman (bass) and Will Champion (drummer), under the now world-famous name of Coldplay.

No one could have foreseen the success of this debut album. Topping the UK charts and selling approximately 8.5 million copies around the world, *Parachutes* was just the beginning for this multi-million selling rock band. With estimated sales so far standing at over 100 million copies worldwide, it is undisputable that Coldplay are one of the most successful British bands of all time.

Performance Notes

Viva La Vida is played at a lively tempo with plenty of syncopation in the melody and accompaniment. It is important to feel four strong beats in each measure to recreate the driving essence of the song. Thinking of the lyrics and vocal melody can help in deciding which notes to accent in order to convey the right feel. In this particular track, Chris Martin (Coldplay vocalist) often chooses to accent the notes on the down beats within each measure, consequently mirroring the steady quarter note pulse that the drums are providing.

The main challenge of the piece will be to start each phrase confidently and to remain in control of the rhythm through the heavily syncopated measures. You must be aware where each phrase starts in the measure and be able to start assertively, as there will be no cue from the accompaniment. There are three points in the song where you will rest for several measures. Count these measures carefully so you do not lose track of the second ukulele part. Play your notes smoothly and make sure the phrases flow to make them sound lyrical.

The melody needs to be played further up the neck in some places. Think about the best position for your fretting hand so you can keep the phrases sounding smooth, particularly during mid-phrase position changes.

You will be developing your own accompaniment during measures 53 to 60. It is marked ***f*** (*forte*) but work carefully with the second ukulele player (or duet part on the accompanying audio) to complement the solo line. Your rhythmic accompaniment should be in a similar style to the syncopated style found in accompaniment elsewhere in the song.

Viva La Vida

Duet

Candidate Part (Assessed)

Coldplay

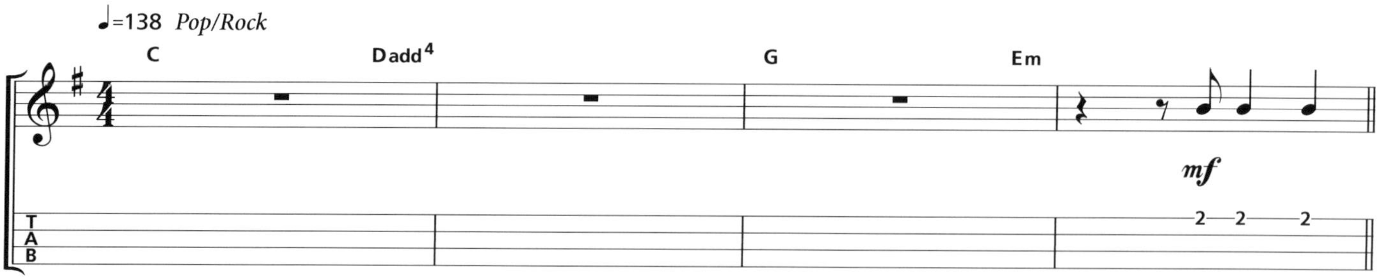

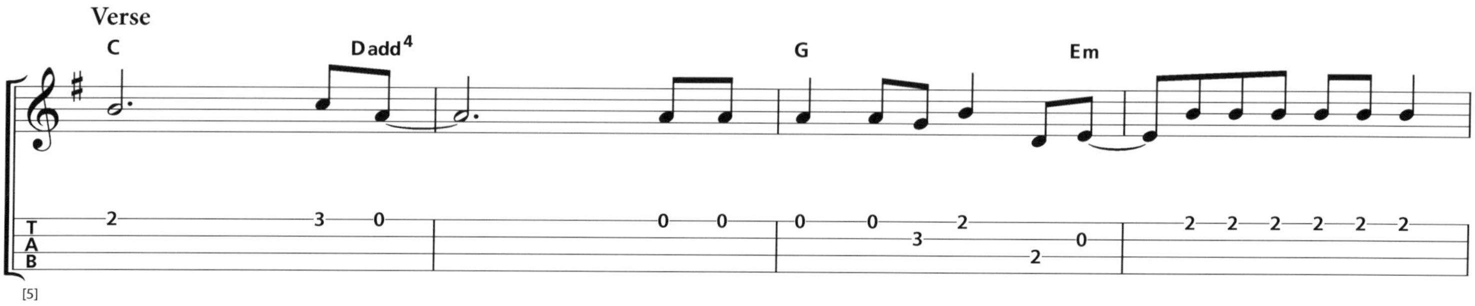

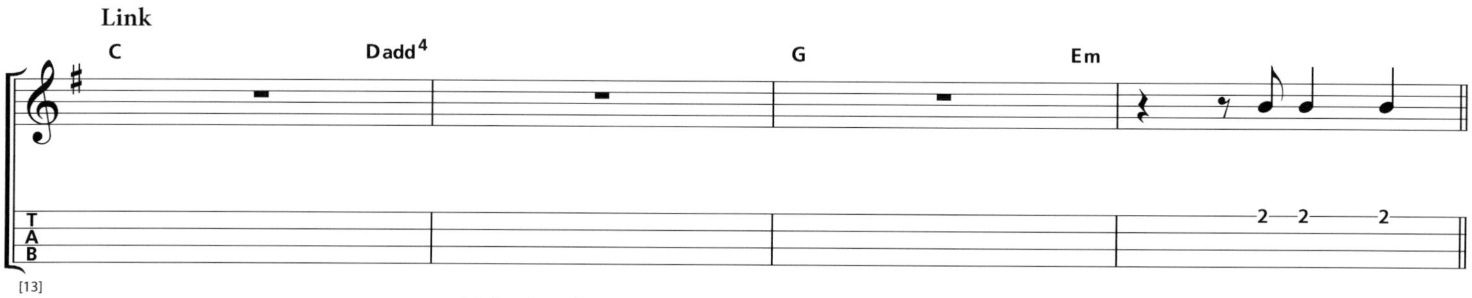

Verse
C
D
G
Em
[17]
C
D
G
Em
[21]
C
D
G
Em
[25]
C
D
G
Em
f
[29]
Chorus
C
D
G
Em
[33]

C D G Em
[37]
C D G Em
[41]
C D G Em
mf
[45]
Link
C Em D
[49]
Refrain
C D G Em
f Develop accompaniment
[53]

C
D
G
Em
[57]
Chorus
C
D
G
Em
[61]
C
D
G
Em
[65]
C
D
G
Em
[69]
C
D
G
Em
dim.
p
[73]

Viva La Vida

Duet

Duet Part (Non-assessed)

Coldplay

Verse
C
Dadd4
G
Em
(PM)
[17]
C
Dadd4
G
Em
(PM)
[21]
C
Dadd4
G
Em
(PM)
[25]
C
D
G
Em
(PM)
[29]
Chorus
C
D
G
Em
[33]

C
D
G
Em
[37]
[41]
mp
[45]
Link
Em
cresc.
f
[49]
Refrain
[53]

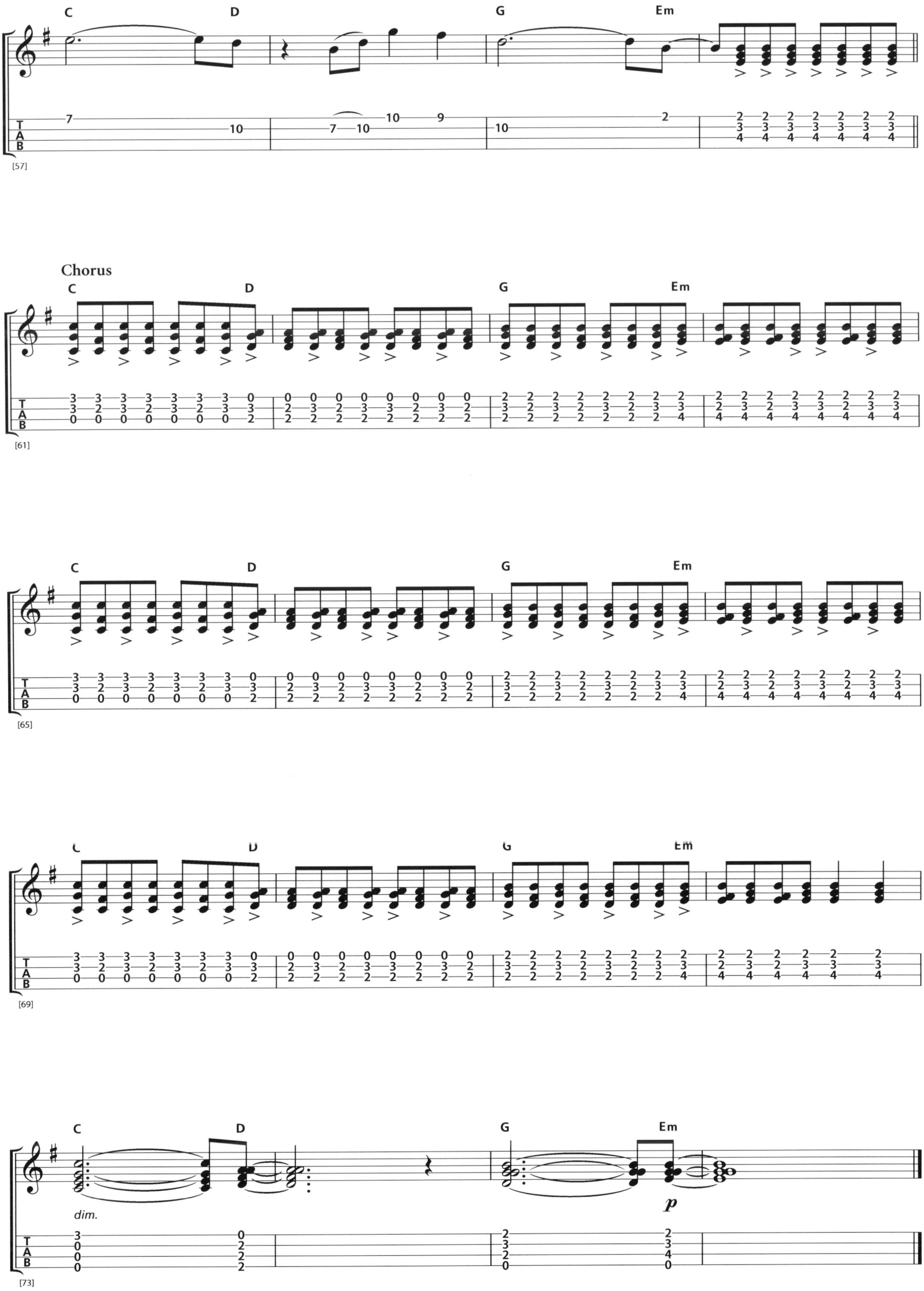
C
D
G
Em
[57]
Chorus
C
D
G
Em
[61]
C
D
G
Em
[65]
C
D
G
Em
[69]
C
D
G
Em
dim.
p
[73]

'California Dreamin'' | The Mamas and the Papas

Album: *If You Can Believe Your Eyes and Ears*
Released: 1965
Label: Dunhill Records
Genre: 60's Pop
Chart Peak: 4 (US)
Written By: John Phillips / Michelle Phillips
Produced By: Lou Adler

Background Info

California Dreamin' was written by husband and wife John and Michelle Phillips in 1963. The pair were members of the group New Journeymen at the time, which later evolved into the well-known multi-million selling act that was The Mamas and the Papas. The track was first recorded by American singer-songwriter Barry McGuire, but it was the later version by The Mamas and the Papas, who incidentally recorded backing vocals for McGuire's version, that became a hit in both the US and the UK.

Released as a single in 1965, 'California Dreamin' failed to take the charts by storm until a Boston based radio station came across the song and began to air it regularly in early 1966. This led to a peak position of number 4 in the US, where it stayed for 17 weeks and was certified gold, and number 23 in the UK. In 1997, Carling Premier used The Mamas and the Papas recording to advertise their lager and saw the song re-enter the charts. This time peaking at the higher spot of number 9 on the UK singles chart. In 2001 'California Dreamin' was inducted into the Grammy Hall of Fame and is ranked at number 89 on Rolling Stone Magazine's list of The 500 Greatest Songs of All Time.

The Mamas and the Papas consisted of John Phillips, Michelle Phillips, Denny Doherty and Cass Elliot. John Phillips, formerly of New Journeymen, was the group's leader and had a vision of bringing folk into the new beat style of the 1960s. Although he had concerns about Cass Elliot joining the group due to her alto, he was overruled by his fellow band members and so the famous line-up was born. Together they released five studio albums and 17 singles before going their separate ways, with three of them embarking on a solo career. Cass Elliot, who had become known as Mama Cass, successfully toured both the US and Europe as a solo artist before sadly losing her life to heart failure in 1974.

Performance Notes

As the title suggests, this arrangement requires a dreamy laid-back feel. The notes in the introduction should over ring where possible, so think carefully about your fingering for the chord shapes in order to create this effect.

The dotted eighth-note rhythms (beats 3 and 4 of measure 1 for example), will need to be treated carefully. Use the audio track as guidance for what this sounds like. Challenging rhythmic patterns can be practised by clapping or singing the rhythm as a first step. Note the slight difference to a triplet sound, where the notes would be spread evenly.

The introduction ends in measure 4 with a chord marked ***sfz***, short for 'sforzando' which means you need to suddenly get loud for this chord. You will also see the upwards arrow telling you we should hear all the individual notes, so press hard but strum/pick slowly.

There are a few chords which will need a half barre in the A section (B♭ in measure 5 for example) but they are mostly open shapes. Watch out for the syncopation of the 'pushed' chords when you change shapes on the final eighth note of the measure. This is an important feature of the song to keep it feeling light and to stop it feeling too steady.

Raise your dynamic level in section B so your solo can be clearly heard over the band. The solo was originally played on flute and the phrasing is very smooth. Imitate this by making sure you hold all your notes for their full value.

Use the chords in the C section to develop your own single note pattern. Hold down the chord shapes and pick out your pattern with an over ringing effect. Move smoothly into section D with a strong rhythmic feel to make the song pick up power for the final section.

California Dreamin′

Session Style

The Mamas and the Papas

B♭ C Asus4 A
if I was in L. A.
Cal - i - for - nia
[14]
Dm C B♭ C
dream - in'
on such a win - ter's
[17]
Asus4 A
day.
[19]
B
Interlude
Dm
[21]
B♭ F A7 Dm B♭
[24]

A7sus4
A7
Dm
C
[27]
B♭
C
A7sus4
A7
[30]
Dm
C
B♭
C
[33]
A7sus4
A7
Stopped in - to a
[35]
C
Dm
C
B♭
C
Asus4
church,
I passed a - long the way.
Develop
mp
[37]

A Bb F A Dm Bb
Oh, I got down on my knees, and I pre - tend to pray.
[40]
Asus4 A
You know the preach - er likes the
[43]
D
Dm C Bb Bb C Asus4
cold. He knows I'm gon - na stay.
mf
[45]
A Dm C Bb Bb C
Cal - i - for - nia dream - in' on such a win - ter's
[48]
Asus4 A Dm
day.
[51]

'Jamming' | Bob Marley

Album: *Exodus*
Released: 1977
Label: Tuff Gong / Island

Genre: Reggae
Written By: Bob Marley
Chart Peak: 20 (US Billboard 200)

Background Info

'Jamming' features as one of six singles from Bob Marley and the Wailers' ninth studio album, *Exodus*. Since its release, it has become one of the most well-known songs within the reggae genre. To many musicians, it is almost viewed as a stylistic blueprint for a reggae song. Its off-beat guitars, lyrical content and percussion can now be considered as symbolic of reggae music. The phrase "jamming" is often thought of as a term to describe people making music together. However, within Jamaican culture it's also used as an even broader term for simply getting together or have a celebration.

The recording of *Exodus* would have taken place in Jamaica. However, in 1976 there was an assassination attempt on Marley which resulted in him relocating to London and recording the album there. Since its recording, the album has received great success both critically and commercially, receiving 'Album of the Century' in 1999 from Time Magazine. Many of its tracks were consequently then used on Marley's greatest hits album, *Legend*, which has become the highest selling reggae album of all time. To date, Bob Marley's records have total estimated sales of over 75 million worldwide.

Following Marley's exile to London, he returned to Jamaica and performed an iconic version of 'Jamming' at the legendary One Love Peace Concert on April 22 1978.

Marley was a committed Rastafarian whose gentle personality, politically and socially conscious lyrics and gift for song writing made for an explosive mix when coupled with the reggae flavour of his native Jamaica. His music gained worldwide appeal in the 70's, particularly after the release of *Exodus*. He is still a renowned and beloved figure in popular culture today.

Performance Notes

This is a classic reggae track with the ukulele part enhancing the feel by emphasising beat 2 and 4 through most of the song. Listen carefully to the band to make sure you are matching the swing feel of the rhythm. The ukulele part must sound laid back but your chords need to be clear and crisp. The minor key is of particular interest because we might expect the song to sound melancholy but the overall style of the song gives it an upbeat feel.

You will need to be confident playing barre chords to perform this song. Your first finger should be straight to perform a successful barre chord so think about your posture and hand position if your chords sound muffled. Most of the chord voicings use all four strings but make sure you also strum carefully when playing the smaller voicings (end of measure 7 for example), as the open strings can clash with your chords.

Muting is a very important technique in the song. Most of the chords are played with only fretted notes. It is possible to mute these chords by relaxing the fretting hand so that the hand is resting on the strings but without enough force that they're pressing onto the frets. However, chords which include open strings are most easily muted with the strumming hand. You may decide it is easier to use this technique throughout the song.

The middle 8 asks for a gradual *crescendo* and *diminuendo*. Practise this smoothly, increasing and decreasing your volume to achieve this swelling effect. You will need to strike the strings clean and hard to play the strong accents in measures 29 and 31.

The ad lib section will give you the opportunity to improvise some answering phrases in the breaks in the vocal line. Start by experimenting with your D major pentatonic scale (this is in the technical section) but with a slight twist: Treat B as the most important note in the scale (second fret on the A string). This transforms the scale from D major pentatonic to B minor pentatonic! These scales are relatives because they have the same notes in them.

Jamming

Session Style

Bob Marley

Words and Music by Bob Marley

Bm7 E7 G F♯m
jam - min' jam - min' and I hope you like jam - min' too Ain't no rules,
[13]
Verse
Bm7 E7 Bm7 E7 G F♯m
ain't no vow, we can do it an - y how I 'n' I will see you through 'Cos e - ve - ry
mp
[17]
Bm7 E7 Bm7 E7 G F♯m
day we pay the price, we're the liv - ing sac - ri - fice Jam - min' till the jam is through
[21]
Middle 8
Bm7 Em7 Bm7
Ho - ly mout Zi - on Ho - ly mout
[25]

Em7 Bm Bm
— Zi - on Jah sit - teth in Mount — Zi - on. and rules — all cre -
sfz sfz
[28]
Bm7 E7
a - tion yeh — we're, — we're jam - min' wot - cha - wa - wa -
mf
[32]
Bm7 E7 G F♯m7
wa We're jam - min' I wan - na jam it with you We're
ad lib. lead fills around vocal lines
[35]
Bm7 E7 G F♯m7
jam - min' I'm jammed, I hope you're jam - min' too Jah
[39]

Verse
Bm7 E7 Bm7 E7 G F♯m
knows how much I tried The truth I can - not hide, to keep you sat - is - fied True
mp
[43]
Bm7 E7 Bm7 E7 G F♯m
love that now ex - ist is the love I can't re - sist so jam by my side We're
[47]
Chorus
Bm7 E7 G
jam - min' I wan - na jam it with you
mp
[51]
F♯m Bm7 E7
We're jam - min' we're jam - min' we're jam - min we're jam - min we're jam - min' we're jam - min' we're jam - min we're jam - min'
[54]
G F♯m Bm7
Hope you like jam - min' too
[57]

'Golden Touch' | Razorlight

Album: *Up All Night*
Released: 2004
Label: Vertigo
Genre: Indie

Written By: Johnny Borrell
Produced by: John Cornfield

Background Info

'Golden Touch' was the fourth single to be released from Razorlight's debut album *Up All Night.* The track peaked at number 9 in the UK and gave Razorlight their first top ten hit. As well as achieving impressive sales, 'Golden Touch' was also met with critical acclaim and was ranked at number 87 on Q Magazine's 2006 list of '100 Greatest Songs Ever'. Various acoustic versions of the track have been released, most notably on Radio 1's 2006 album *Live Lounge*. The performances are often bolstered with the addition of a female choir, providing an excellent alternative to the original and one which should absolutely be listened to by fans of the song.

Razorlight's album, *Up All Night,* saw the band launch into commercial success and gave them three top 20 UK singles, including a number 2 hit with 'Somewhere Else'. The album peaked at number 3 in the UK and achieved 4 x platinum status with sales of over 1.2 million copies. This was quite an accomplishment for the London based indie band's debut album, but it was only the beginning. In 2006 they released their second studio album, *Razorlight,* which topped the UK album chart and saw the group achieve their first UK number one single with 'America'. The self-titled record was awarded 3 x platinum status in Ireland and 5 x platinum status in their home country, with sales of over 1.5 million copies. In 2008 the band continued their streak of top 5 albums when their third release, *Slipway Fires,* peaked at number 4 in the UK.

Razorlight formed in London in 2002 and after several line-up changes now consist of Johnny Borrell (lead vocals/guitar), Björn Ågren (guitar), Reni Lane (keyboard), Ben Ellis (bass) and Mat Hector (drums). After the release of their third studio album, tensions were high and many original members found themselves going in a different direction. This eventually led to a split in 2014, with no releases between the years of 2008 and then. In 2018 the band resurfaced with the line-up detailed above and released their fourth studio album *Olympus Sleeping.* Although the record is yet to achieve the success of its predecessors, peaking at number 27 some years after the height of British Indie Rock is still quite the victory.

Performance Notes

The opening measures of Golden Touch contain 'cue' notes (played by the electric guitar on the backing track). These indicate to us what we can expect to hear during the first two measures after the count in, before the ukulele part begins at measure 3.

This arrangement contains a variety of interesting accompaniment techniques which, when mastered, make for an exciting performance. In the verse section, we see a variety of barre chord shapes which should be learnt in isolation before attempting the full part. The strumming is best executed with down-strums on the eighth notes, allowing for an up-strum where 16th note rhythms occur. Note also that the chords must have a 'choppy' feel (shown by the *staccato* articulations). This can be achieved by slightly lifting the fretting hand away from the fingerboard between each chord, but remaining in contact with the strings.

The chorus arpeggios should ring out wherever possible, and care will be needed with both picking and fretting hands here to be secure with positioning. We also see some 'spread' chord indications (e.g. measure 21, measure 22): this tells us that the chords should be strummed a little more slowly so that each note can be just heard in isolation.

Finally, be sure to leave enough 'headroom' in the overall dynamic so you are able to achieve accents where shown on the chords from measure 33 onwards. These should be strong, but not too forced.

Golden Touch

Session Style

Razorlight

C♯m
much.
But then all
[11]
Chorus
C♯m B F♯m A
they know is how to put you down. When you're there,
let ring
[13]
C♯m B F♯m A
they're your friend; but then, when you're not a - round, they say "Oh,
[15]
C♯m B F♯m A
she's changed." You know what they mean: well, they mean
[17]
C♯m B F♯m A C♯m
they're just jea-lous, be-cause they nev - er do the things they wish that they could do so well.
[19]

Verse
A
G♯m
C♯m
F♯m
G♯m
That kind of girl, yes, she's nev - er a - lone.
You leave a thou - sand mes - sa - ges on her phone.
[23]
C♯m
E
G♯m/D♯
C♯m
But you know you nev - er get through.
[26]
F♯m
G♯m
F♯m
G♯m
And you could have it all if you want it, girl;
and you could have it all if it mat - ters to you.
[29]
C♯m
But then all
[31]
Chorus
C♯m
B
F♯m
G♯m
they know is how to put you down..
When you're there,
[33]

C♯m B F♯m G♯m
they're your friend; but then, when you're not a - round, they say "Oh,
[35]
C♯m B F♯m G♯m
she's changed." You know what they mean: well, they mean
[37]
C♯m B F♯m G♯m
they're just jea - lous, be - cause they nev - er do the things they wish that they could do so
[39]
C♯m F♯m G♯m
well. No, they'll nev - er so the things that they wish that they could do so
[41]
C♯m F♯m G♯m C♯m
well. No, they'll nev - er so the things that they wish that they could do so well.
[43]

'Dreaming' | Imelda May

Album: *Tribal*
Released: 2014
Label: Decca

Genre: Rockabilly
Written By: Chris Stein / Debbie Harry
Produced By: Mike Crossey / Imelda May

Background Info

Imelda May's 2014 cover of the Blondie classic 'Dreaming' features just ukulele and vocals and features on May's fourth studio album *Tribal*. The beautifully stripped back version of Blondie's hit has been highly commended by critics, with many feeling that singer May was genius to recognise the potential for a ballad/ukulele cover of the original and that the simplicity of her recording only solidifies the strength of Harry and Stein's song writing. To perform a song with only a vocal and a ukulele leaves no space for hiding poor lyrics or melody, and May's version certainly highlights stunning lines such as 'dreaming is free' and 'we just keep on dreaming'. This stripped back version of the 80s classic gives the listener the chance to really appreciate May's wonderful vocal performance, as she delivers a mesmerizing and sincere cover of the power pop song.

Imelda May is an Irish singer-songwriter and multi-instrumentalist, known for her revival of rockabilly and often compared to jazz legends such as Billie Holiday, her spectacular vocals highly admired by many. She has released five studio albums since her launch in 2003 and continues to be hailed a music ambassador in her home country of Ireland, where she hosts 'The Imelda May Show' (showcasing the best of up and coming Irish artists) and works alongside Dublin's BIMM music college to provide a scholarship (named after her).

'Dreaming' was first released in 1979 as the lead single from *Eat to the Beat,* the fourth studio album from new wave legends Blondie. The original single charted in over 10 countries worldwide, peaking at number 27 on the US Billboard Hot 100 and number 2 on the UK singles chart. *Eat to the Beat* topped the UK album chart on its release, and although it only peaked at number 17 on the US album chart it did remain there for a year and so became one of the biggest selling Billboard albums of 1980.

Blondie released their self-titled debut studio album in 1976; they quickly became known for their ability to merge genres such as disco, pop and reggae (to name a few) and were soon a household name in the UK. However, it wasn't until their third studio release, *Parallel Lines (1978,) that* they managed to break the US commercial market. Between the years of 1976 and 1982 the band released six studio albums, all of which charted in the UK, before disbanding with lead vocalist Debbie Harry going on to establish a solo career. 1997 saw the re-formation of Blondie followed by another top ten album in 1999, with the release of *No Exit*. To this day they continue to write, record and tour together and have released a total of 11 studio albums across five decades.

Performance Notes

This arrangement is based on Imelda May's beautiful version of Dreaming, which features a vocal accompanied by a ukulele. The rhythmic feel is very important here; you should play a relaxed shuffle by swinging the 16th notes and accenting the off-beat eighth notes. The key of C major makes the chord shapes and melody feel comfortable on the ukulele and also adds to the mild, peaceful feel.

The melody line often appears within the ukulele chord voicings. Listen carefully to the singer to make sure your phrases match the vocal line. You will need to think about your fingering when fretting chords so you can change shapes smoothly and easily.

The dynamic changes are an important part of the song structure. An interesting feature of this piece is that the chorus should be played at a lower dynamic than the verse to highlight the relaxed feel of the song.

You can develop your own choice of chord voicing and rhythms in the middle 8. Look back at what has been used already but note that this section should be played ***f*** *(forte)*, so it should feel like a livelier section of the song.

Dreaming

Session Style

Imelda May

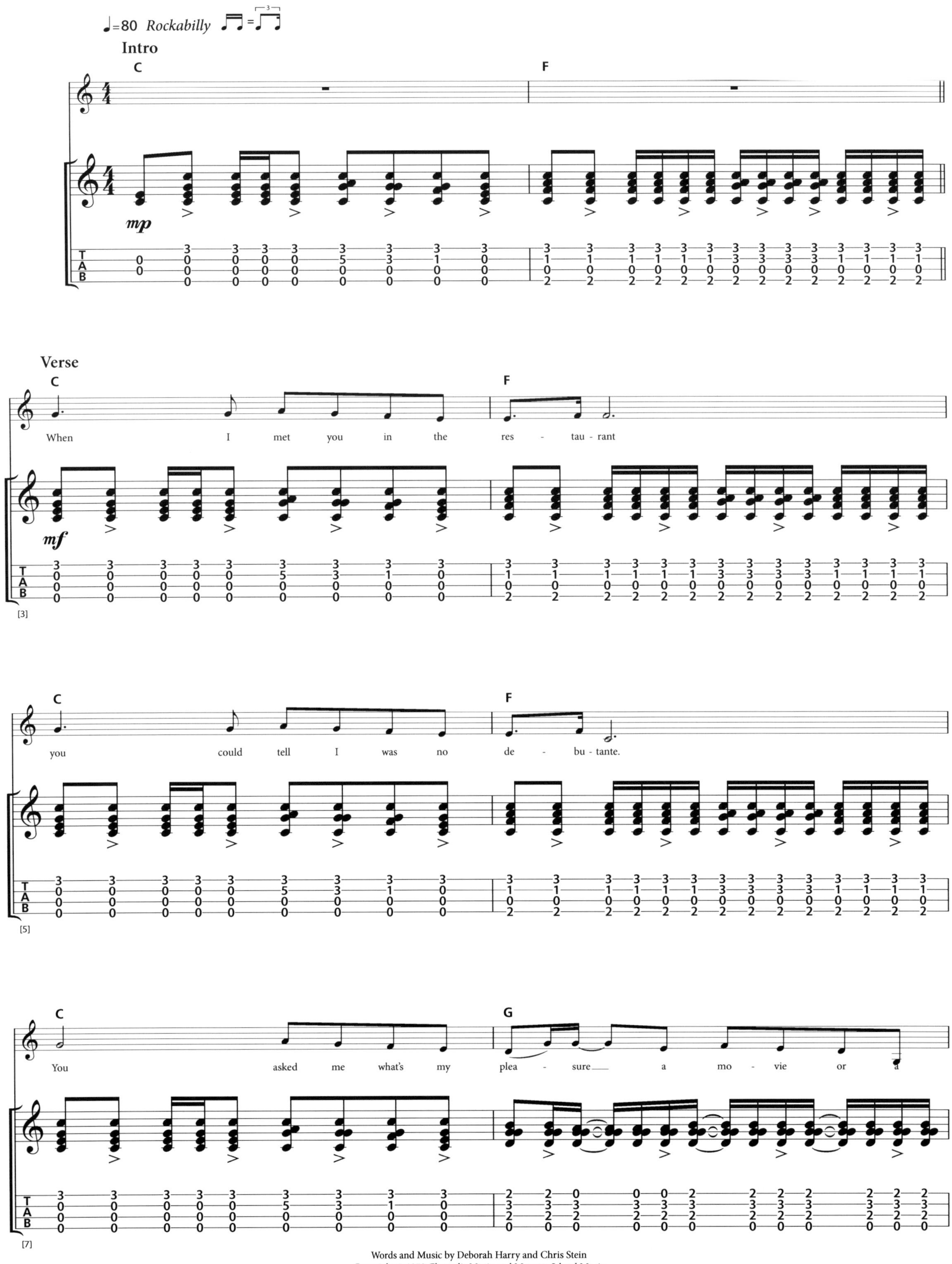

Words and Music by Deborah Harry and Chris Stein

Am
F
mea - sure? I'll have a cup of tea and tell you of my
[9]
Chorus
C
F
drea - ming, drea - ming is free
mp
[11]
C
F
drea - ming drea - ming is free
[13]
Middle 8
F
C
beat feet wal - king a two mile meet me meet me at the turn - stile I ne - ver met him I'll
f cont. sim.
[15]

G
ne - ver for - get him
F
dream dream ev - en for a lit - tle while
dream dream fil - ling up an i - dle hour
[18]
C
fade a - way
G
ra - di - ate
G7
[21]
Verse
C
I sit by and watch the
F
ri - ver flow
mf
[24]
C
I sit by and watch the
F
traf - fic go I -
[26]
C
ma - gine some - thing of your
G
ve - ry own some - thing you can
[28]

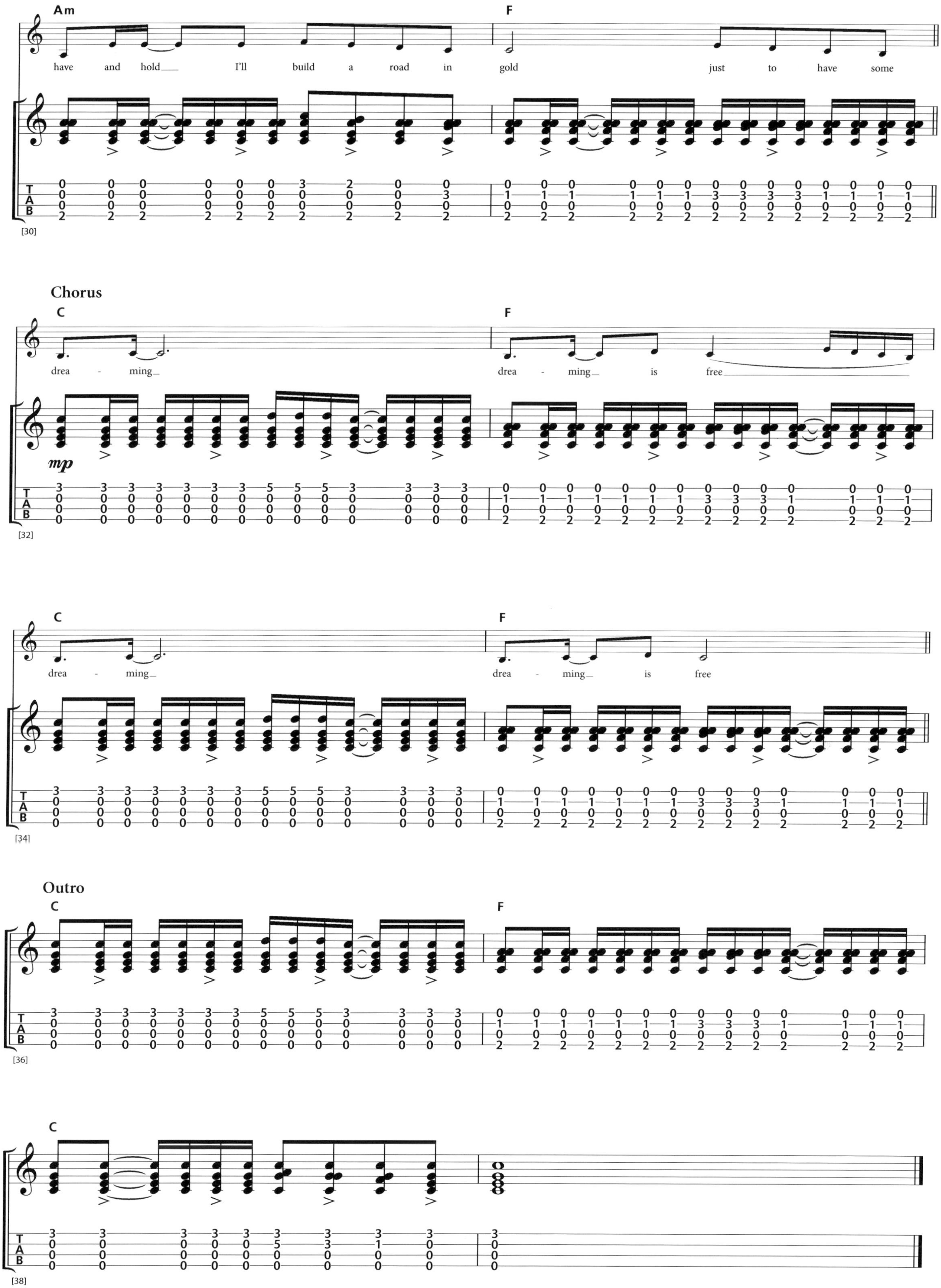

Am
F
have and hold I'll build a road in gold just to have some
[30]
Chorus
C
F
drea - ming
drea - ming is free
mp
[32]
C
F
drea - ming
drea - ming is free
[34]
Outro
C
F
[36]
C
[38]

Technical Exercises

At Level/Grade 3 you will be required to play a selection of exercises drawn from each of the groups below.

All exercises need to be played with a straight feel, using the given rhythmic values at the tempos shown.

Note that Groups A and B need to be played to a click. Group C need to be played as indicated in each example.

Group A | Scales
The tempo for this group is ♩=90 bpm.

Exercises 1–4 need to be prepared from the root notes D, E♭ and E

1. Major (E♭ major shown)

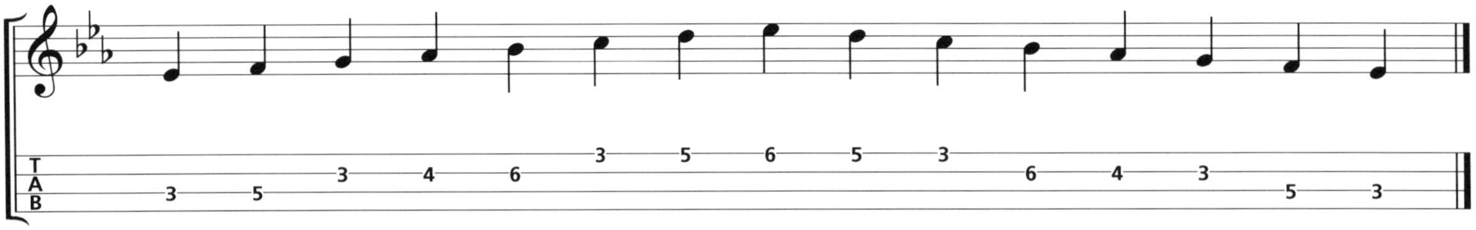

2. Natural minor (D natural minor shown)

3. Major pentatonic (E major pentatonic shown)

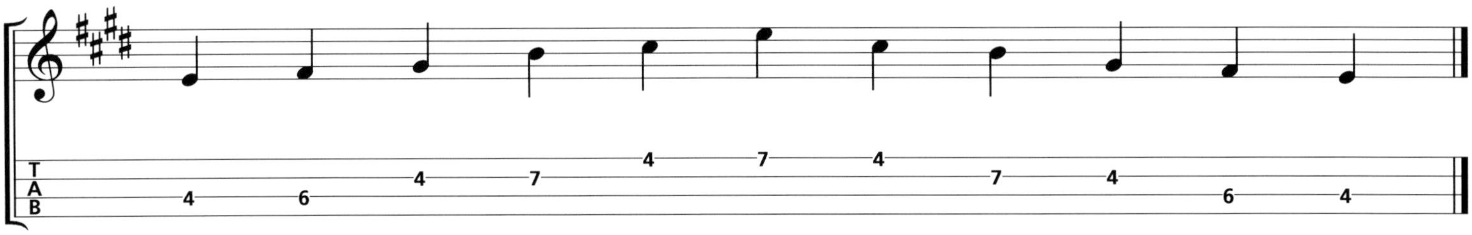

4. Minor pentatonic (D minor pentatonic shown)

Exercises 5 & 6 need to be prepared in the keys shown only, with the given fingering

5. C major pentatonic | campanella style

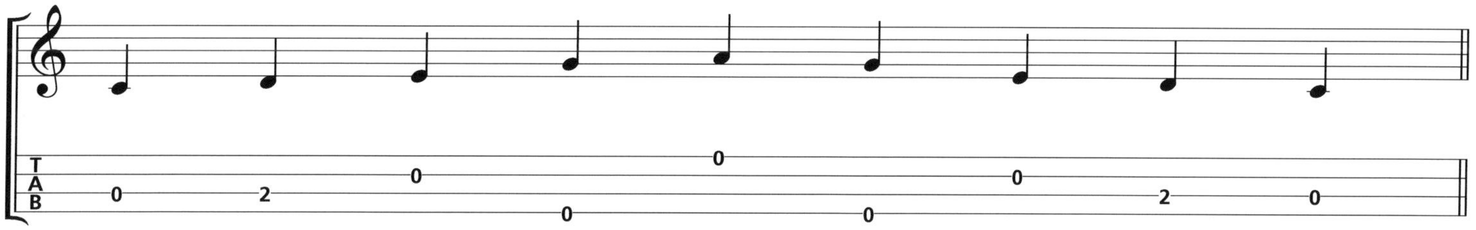

6. C major | linear pattern on 3rd string

Group B | Arpeggios

The tempo for this group is ♩=90 bpm.

Exercises 1–3 need to be prepared from the root notes D, E♭ and E

1. Major (D major shown)

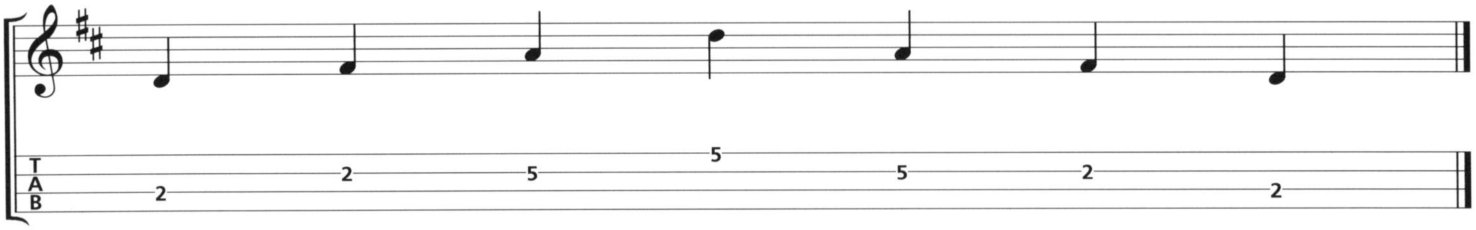

2. Minor (E minor shown)

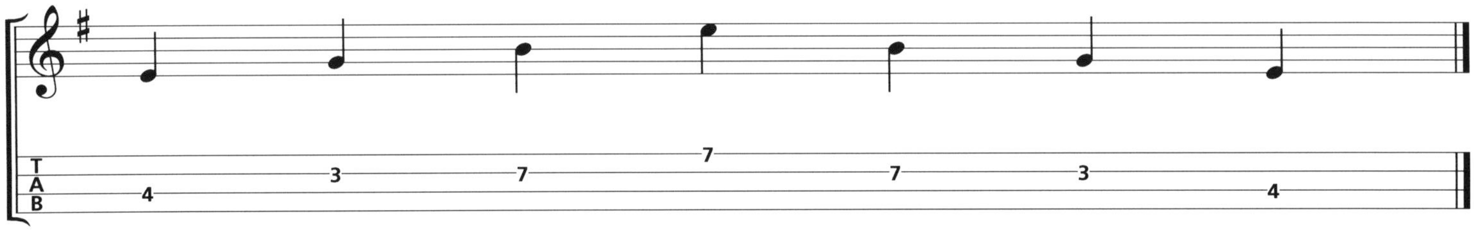

3. Diminished (D diminished shown)

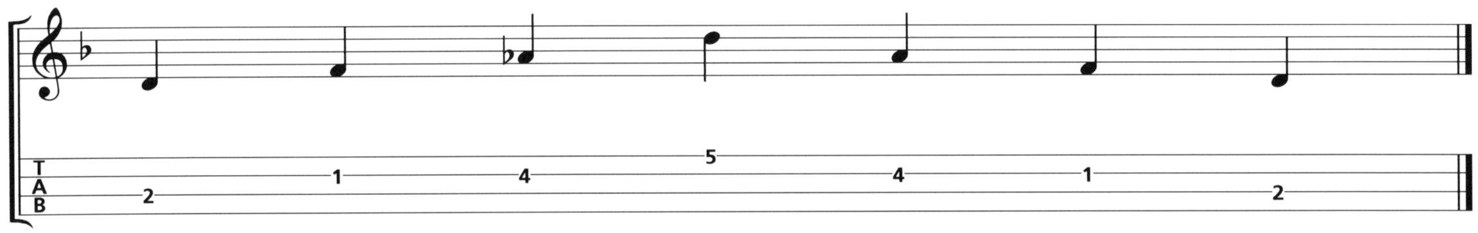

Exercises 4 & 5 need to be prepared in the keys shown only, using the given fingering

4. D major arpeggio on four strings

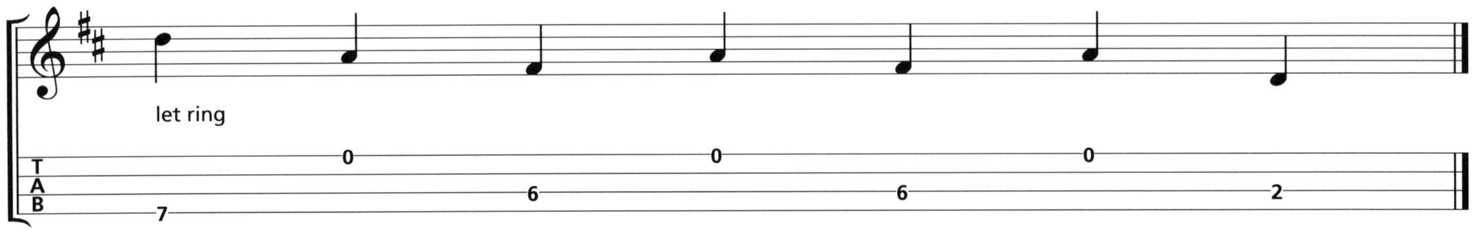

5. E major arpeggio on four strings

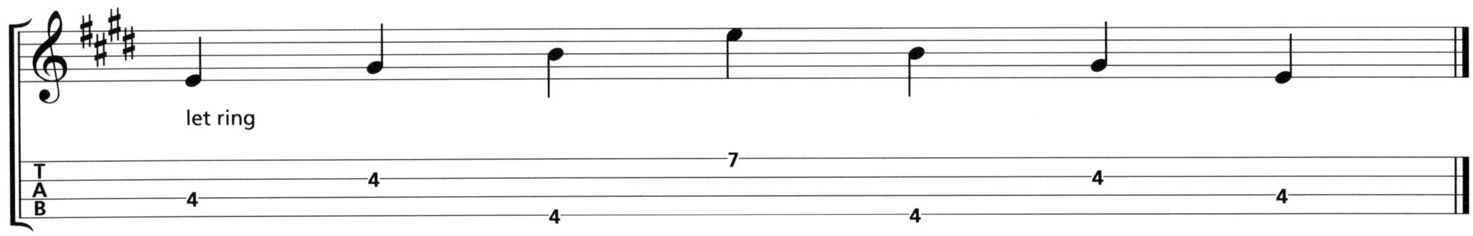

Group C | Chords

Exercises 1 & 2 need to be prepared in the keys of D, E♭ and E.

Exercise 3 need to be prepared in the key shown only.

1. Diminished triads | Two inversions to be played in the key of D, E♭ or E (D shown)

When announced by the assessor, candidates must demonstrate both inversions in the key stated.

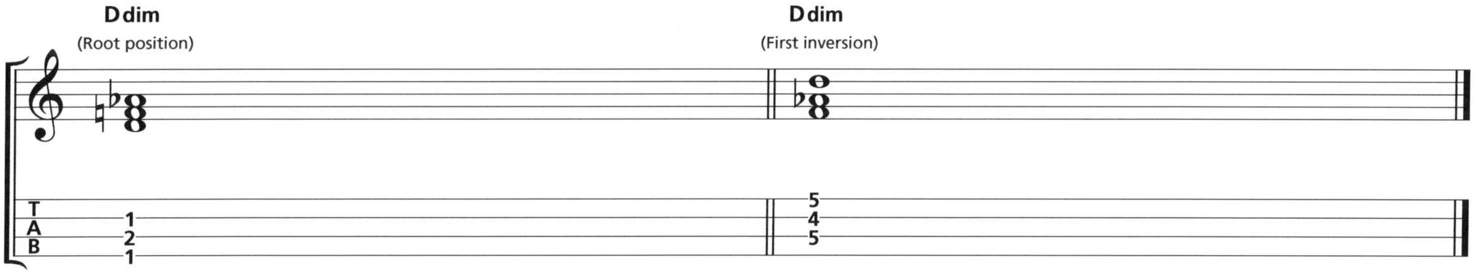

2. Barre Chords in the key of D, E♭ or E (D shown) | Chord shapes to be played in sequence to continuous click

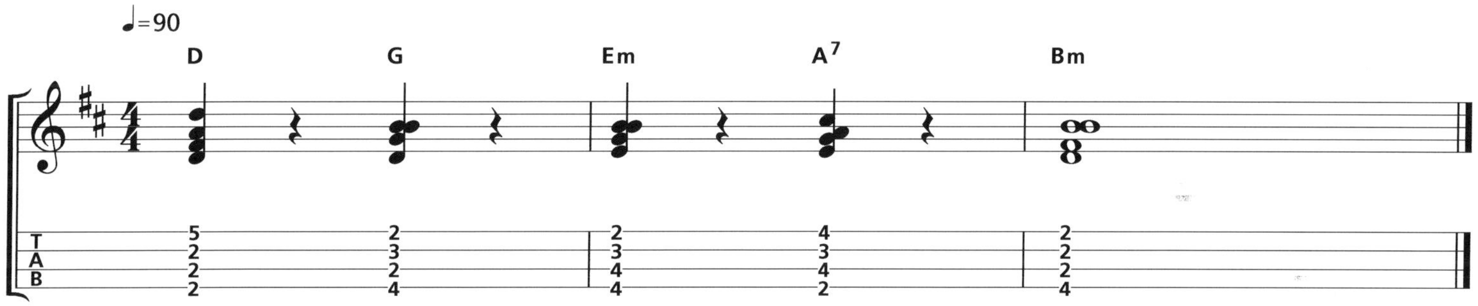

3. Strumming exercise exercise in B minor | Chordal muting and groove exercise to be played to continuous click

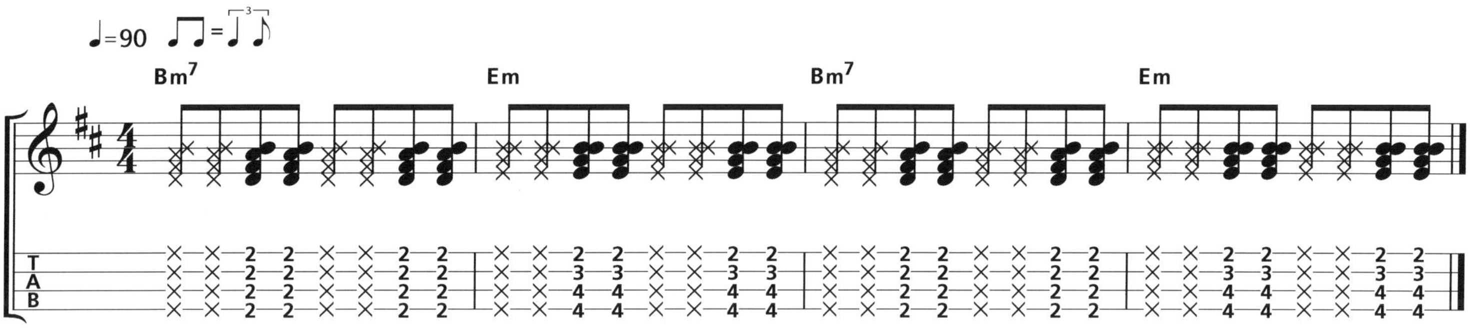

Supporting Tests

Section 1 | Sight Reading

In the assessment, you have a choice between either a Sight Reading test or an Improvisation & Interpretation test within Section 1. The assessor will ask you which one you wish to choose before commencing. Once you have decided, you cannot change your mind.

In the Sight Reading test, the assessor will give you a four measure melody. You will first be given 90 seconds to practise, after which the assessor will play the backing track twice. The first time is for you to practise and the second time is for you to perform the final version for the assessment. For the first playthrough, the backing track will begin with four clicks. For the second playthrough, there will be a one measure count-in. The tempo is ♩= 80.

During the practice time, you will be given the choice of a metronome click throughout or a one measure count-in at the beginning. The backing track is continuous, so once the first playthrough has finished, the count-in of the second playing will start immediately.

Tempo: ♩= 80
Duration: 4 Measures
Rhythms: Quarter notes and quarter note rests, eighth notes and eighth-note rests
Key: E♭ major or E minor

Please note: exercises may be performed either fingerstyle or with a plectrum.

Example 1

Example 2

Please note: The tests shown are examples: The assessor will give you a different version in the assessment

Section 1 | Improvisation & Interpretation

In the assessment, you have a choice between either a Sight Reading test or an Improvisation & Interpretation test within Section 1. The assessor will ask you which one you wish to choose before commencing. Once you have decided, you cannot change your mind.

In the Improvisation & Interpretation test, the assessor will give you a four measure chord progression in the key of E♭ major or E minor. You will first be given 90 seconds to practise, after which the assessor will play the backing track twice. The first time is for you to practise and the second time is for you to perform the final version for the assessment. For the first playthrough, the backing track will begin with four clicks. For the second playthrough, there will be a one measure count-in. The tempo is ♩= 80–90.

During the practice time, you will be given the choice of a metronome click throughout or a one measure count-in at the beginning.

The backing track is continuous, so once the first playthrough has finished, the count-in of the second playing will start immediately.

At Level/Grade 3, you only need to improvise single note melodies in the key of E♭ major or E minor. The chord symbols show the chord progression of the backing track only.

Example 1

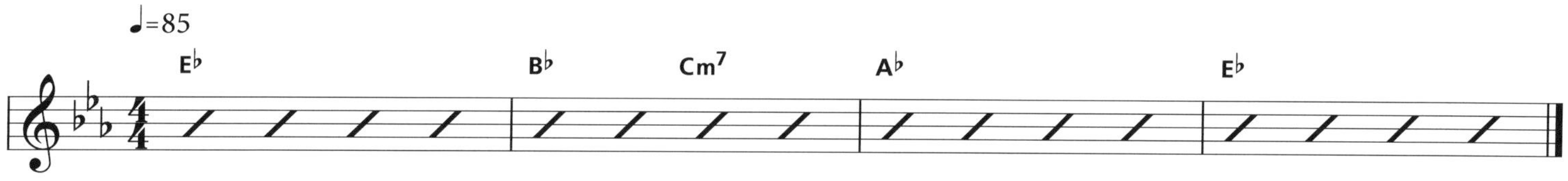

Example 2

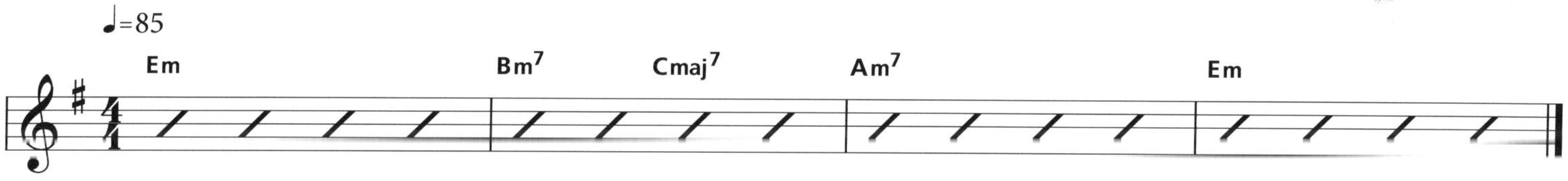

Please note: The tests shown are examples: The assessor will give you a different version in the assessment

Section 2 | Ear Tests

There are two Ear Tests in this level/grade. The assessor will play each test to you twice. You will find one example of each type of test printed below.

Test 1: Melodic Recall

The assessor will play you a two measure melody with a drum backing using the D minor pentatonic scale. The first note of the melody will be the root note and the first interval will be ascending. You will play the melody back on your instrument. You will hear the test twice.

Each time the test is played it is preceded by a one measure count-in. There will be a short gap for you to practise. Next you will hear a vocal count-in and you will then play the melody to the drum backing. The tempo is ♩=85.

♩=85

Test 2: Rhythmic Recall

The assessor will play you a two measure rhythm played to a drum backing on the high A string. You will hear the test twice. You will be asked to play the rhythm back. You will then be asked to identify the rhythm from two printed examples shown to you.

Each time the test is played it is preceded by four clicks. There will be a short gap for you to practise. Next you will hear a vocal count-in and you will then play the rhythm to the drum backing. The tempo is ♩=90.

♩=90

A

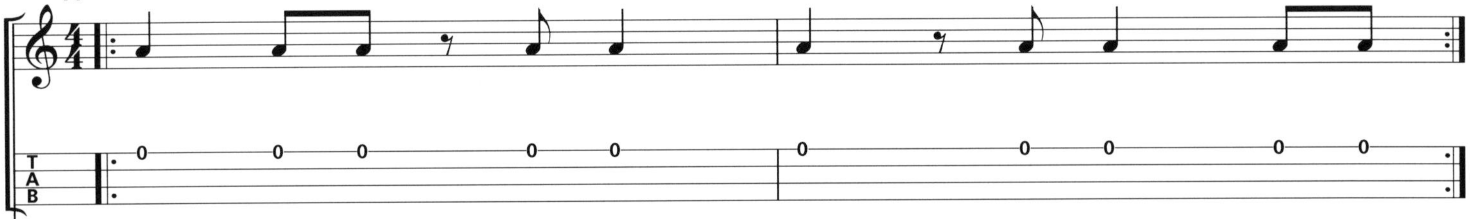

B

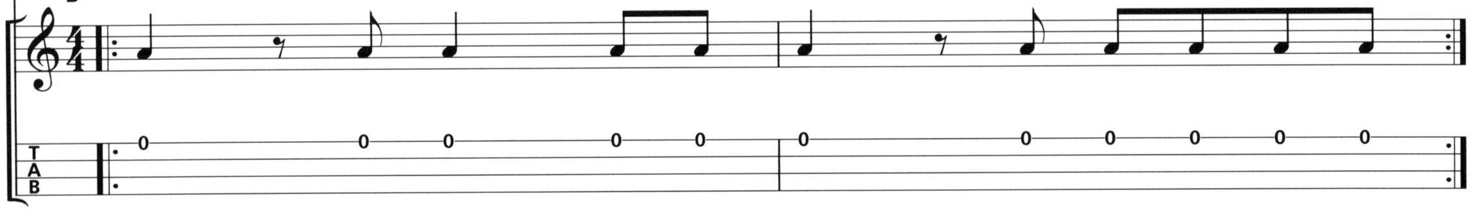

Please note: The test shown is an example: The assessor will give you a different version in the assessment

Section 3 | General Musicianship Questions

The final part of your assessment is the General Musicianship Questions section, which features five questions: four relating to one performance piece of your choosing and one relating to your instrument.

Music Knowledge
The assessor will ask you four music knowledge questions based on a piece of music that you have played in the assessment. You will nominate the piece of music about which the questions will be asked.

In Level/Grade 3 you will be asked to identify:

- The pitch name of notes
- The meaning of the time signature marking
- Whole, half, dotted half, quarter, dotted quarter, eighth and 16th note and rest values
- The construction of any chord found within your piece from the following types:

  Major, minor, sus^4, $dominant^7$, $minor^7$

- The meaning of any dynamic or articulation markings shown on the score

Instrument Knowledge
The assessor will also ask you one question regarding your instrument.

In Level/Grade 3 you will be asked to:

- Identify three of the following parts of your ukulele: neck, fretboard, body, tuning-pegs, nut, soundhole, or bridge
- Identify names of all open strings

About Rockschool Assessments

Entering Rockschool Assessments

Entering a Rockschool assessment is easy, just go online and follow our simple six step process. All details for entering online, dates, fees, regulations and Free Choice Pieces can be found at *www.rslawards.com*

- All candidates should ensure they bring their own Level/Grade syllabus book to the assessment or have proof of digital purchase ready to show the assessor.

Syllabus Guides

You can find further details about Rockschool's Ukulele syllabus by downloading the syllabus guide from our website: *www.rslawards.com*

All candidates should download and read the accompanying syllabus guide when using this level/grade book. Please note that clarifications and updates to syllabus guides are noted at the back of each document.

Performance and Technical Guidance

Students, candidates and teachers may find the following guidance helpful in using the level/grade book and preparing for a Rockschool assessment. Please see below.

- **Tuning**
  Pieces and technical tests have been arranged for re-entrant tuned ukuleles. This is specifically to prepare for the specific techniques which build through the syllabus. If you wish to take a Rockschool assessment using an alternative standard tuning, please contact Rockschool.

- **Fingering**
  Any fingering annotation is given as a guide only. Tablature positions are also given for guidance, except where stipulated to achieve the required technical outcomes (for example, in *campanella* passages).

- **Interpretation**
  Notation should be performed as written, except where there are performance indications to *ad lib. / improvise / develop*, etc. In these instances, the candidate will be marked on their ability to interpret the music in a stylistically appropriate way, commensurate with the level/grade.

- **Adaptation**
  A small degree of adaptation is allowed where, for example, hand stretches do not facilitate the required notated parts. Marks may be deducted if adaptation results in over-simplification of the notation. If in doubt you can submit any adaptation enquiries to: *info@rslawards.com*
  Further adaptation (for example, alternative solos) will be marked according to the equivalent outcomes achieved.

- **Articulation & Dynamics**
  Where articulation and dynamics are marked on the notation, they should be followed. Where it is open to interpretation, the candidate is free to take their own approach, in accordance with the style of the piece.

- **Chord Symbols**
  Most Hit Tune arrangements have chord symbols written above the notation. This is purely for guidance, and to assist the candidate and teacher, and can be used to help inform ideas for development/improvisation sections.

Marking Schemes

Debut to Level/Grade 5 *

ELEMENT	PASS	MERIT	DISTINCTION
Performance Piece 1	12–14 out of 20	15–17 out of 20	18+ out of 20
Performance Piece 2	12–14 out of 20	15–17 out of 20	18+ out of 20
Performance Piece 3	12–14 out of 20	15–17 out of 20	18+ out of 20
Technical Exercises	9–10 out of 15	11–12 out of 15	13+ out of 15
Sight Reading *or* Improvisation & Interpretation	6 out of 10	7–8 out of 10	9+ out of 10
Ear Tests	6 out of 10	7–8 out of 10	9+ out of 10
General Musicianship Questions	3 out of 5	4 out of 5	5 out of 5
TOTAL MARKS	**60%+**	**74%+**	**90%+**

Levels/Grades 6–8

ELEMENT	PASS	MERIT	DISTINCTION
Performance Piece 1	12–14 out of 20	15–17 out of 20	18+ out of 20
Performance Piece 2	12–14 out of 20	15–17 out of 20	18+ out of 20
Performance Piece 3	12–14 out of 20	15–17 out of 20	18+ out of 20
Technical Exercises	9–10 out of 15	11–12 out of 15	13+ out of 15
Quick Study Piece	6 out of 10	7–8 out of 10	9+ out of 10
Ear Tests	6 out of 10	7–8 out of 10	9+ out of 10
General Musicianship Questions	3 out of 5	4 out of 5	5 out of 5
TOTAL MARKS	**60%+**	**74%+**	**90%+**

Performance Certificates | Debut to Level/Grade 8 *

ELEMENT	PASS	MERIT	DISTINCTION
Performance Piece 1	12–14 out of 20	15–17 out of 20	18+ out of 20
Performance Piece 2	12–14 out of 20	15–17 out of 20	18+ out of 20
Performance Piece 3	12–14 out of 20	15–17 out of 20	18+ out of 20
Performance Piece 4	12–14 out of 20	15–17 out of 20	18+ out of 20
Performance Piece 5	12–14 out of 20	15–17 out of 20	18+ out of 20
TOTAL MARKS	**60%+**	**75%+**	**90%+**

* Note that there are no Debut Vocal assessments.

Ukulele Notation Explained

THE MUSICAL STAVE shows pitches and rhythms and is divided by lines into measures. Pitches are named after the first seven letters of the alphabet.

TABLATURE graphically represents the ukulele fingerboard. Each horizontal line represents a string, and each number represents a fret.

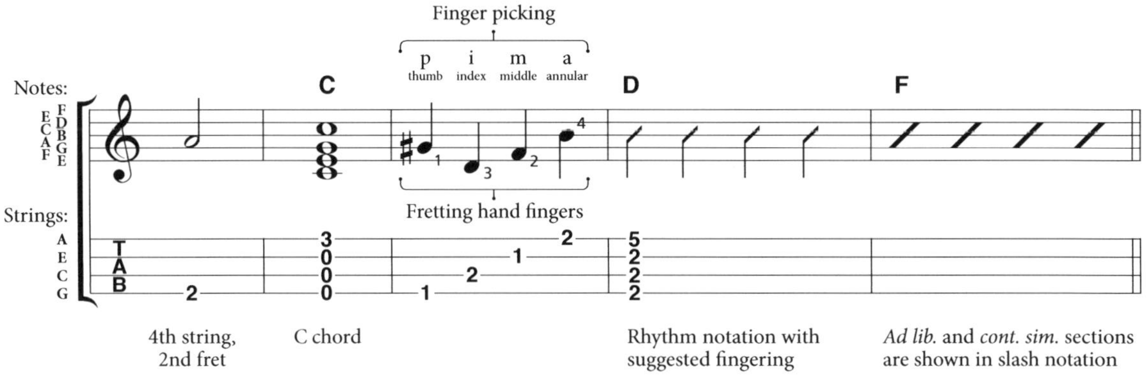

Definitions For Ukulele Notation

HAMMER-ON: Play the lower note, then sound the higher note by fretting it without repicking.

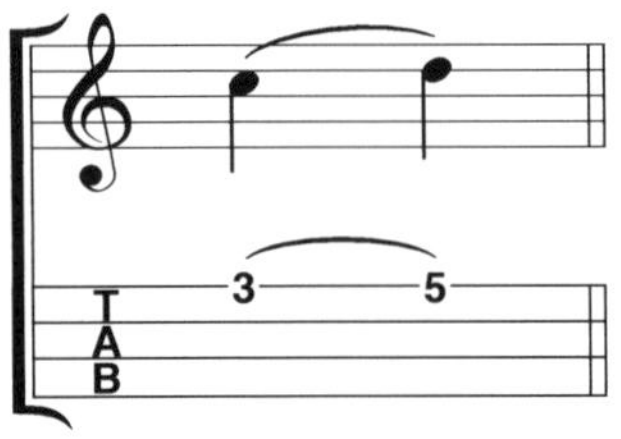

PULL-OFF: Play the higher note then sound the lower note by lifting the finger without repicking.

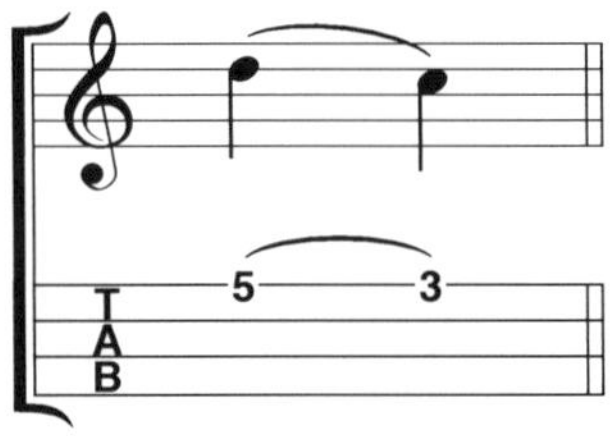

SLIDE: Play the first note, then slide to the next with the same finger.

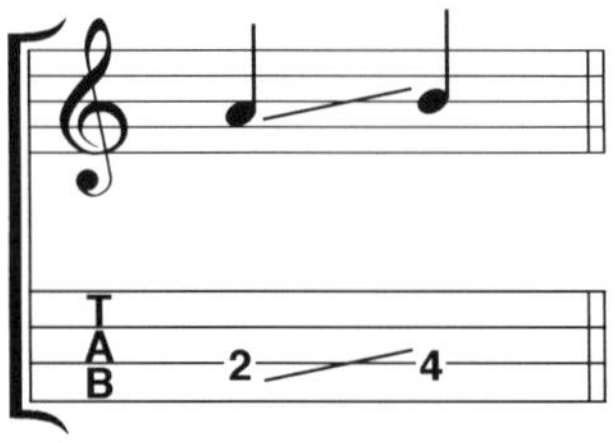

STRING BENDS: Play the first note then bend up or bend down (release the bend) to the pitch indicated in brackets.

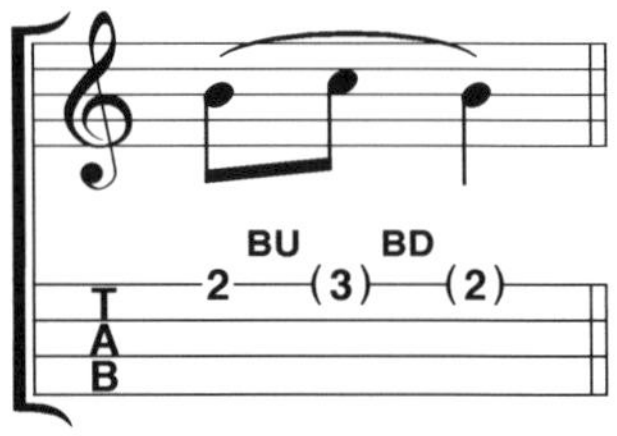

GLISSANDO: A small slide off of a note toward the end of its rhythmic duration. Do not slide 'into' the following note – subsequent notes should be repicked.

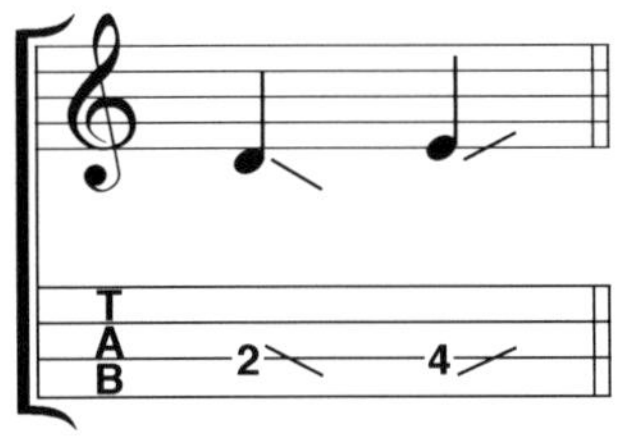

DOWNSTROKE: When using a pick, this symbol indicates a downstroke.

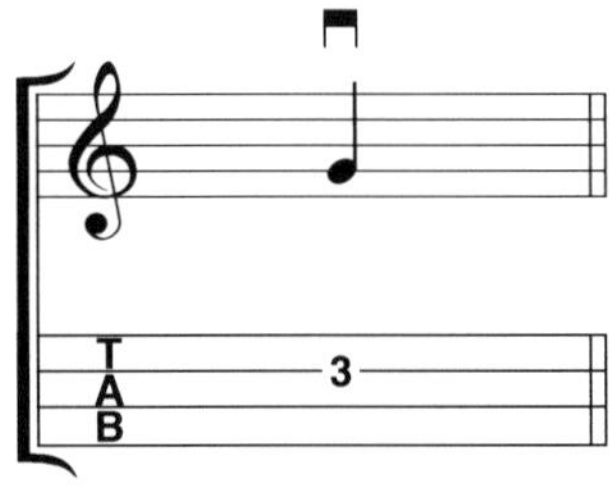

UPSTROKE: When using a pick, this symbol indicates an upstroke.

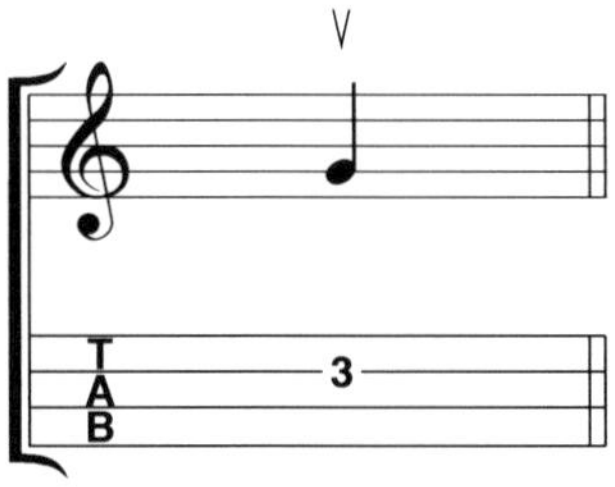

D.𝄋. al Coda

- Go back to the sign (𝄋), then play until the measure marked ***To Coda*** 𝄌 then skip to the section marked 𝄌 ***Coda***.

D.C. al Fine

- Go back to the beginning of the song and play until the measure marked ***Fine*** (end).

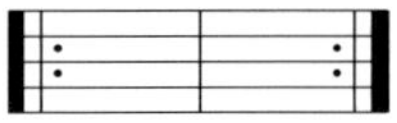

- Repeat the measures between the repeat signs.

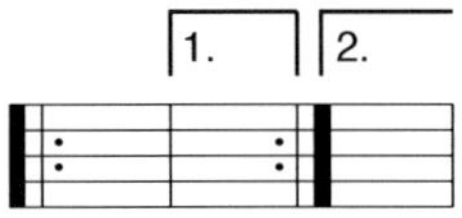

- When a repeated section has different endings, play the first ending only the first time and the second ending only the second time.

Copyright Information